Published on behalf of Glasgow
1999: UK City of Architecture
and Design, by:

August
116–120 Golden Lane
London EC1Y OTL
+44 171 689 4400
mail@augustmedia.co.uk

ISBN: 1–902854–04–7

Glasgow 1999
UK City of Architecture and
Design
Charlotte House
78 Queen Street
Glasgow G1 3DN
+44 141 287 7346
info@glasgow1999.co.uk

Photography:
all photographs by Alan
Dimmick unless otherwise
stated

Cover photograph:
© Alan Dimmick

Picture acknowledgements:
Pages 10, 24, 25, 34, 38 courtesy
The Mitchell Library.
Page 42 courtesy Page and Park
Architects

Series editor: Sarah Gaventa,
Communications Director,
Glasgow 1999
Editor: Jessica Lack
Art director: Stephen Coates
Designer: Anne Odling-Smee
Copy editors: Ally Ireson,
Alex Stetter

Contributors:
Simon Grant
Irene Maver
Texts © the authors

Production co-ordinated by:
Uwe Kraus GmbH
Printed in Italy

Project descriptions
by Simon Grant.
Historical contexts
by Irene Maver.

Preface

Glasgow's people have pioneered new techniques in the regeneration of their city. Its vigorous housing association movement has over the past twenty years moved from the rehabilitation of the tenements to the construction of imaginative new housing. The next step is to address the landscape beyond the threshold of individual homes.

A city is made up not just of its individual buildings, but of its urban landscapes. They provide the landmarks that give shape and grain to a city. They provide a sense of identity. They help to define a sense of community. Glasgow's centre, with its strong urban grid pattern and its characteristic squares, is more than usually well endowed with such landmarks. As it grew in the nineteenth century, its new industrial and residential suburbs were focused on a series of symbolic gateways that tried to bring some of the same qualities of the city's centre to its periphery. And it is this periphery which has subsequently suffered most from a lack of such urban qualities, as shifts in the economic climate have destroyed established communities.

The Five Spaces project was an exploration of the possibility of bringing art, architecture and landscape together to create new places that could provide a focus in the contemporary landscape. The intention was to work with the housing associations to identify spaces that could help support wider regeneration efforts. The first move had to come from the community itself, in identifying suitable sites. We were looking for areas in which there had already been some progress in refurbishing the housing stock, and to achieve a city-wide spread of projects.

The idea of working with the urban landscape was one that Barcelona had explored from the end of the 1980s onward, and Glasgow 1999 arranged for a group of Glaswegians to visit the city. It was a process that gave them a sense of the potential of what could be achieved, but also how much Glasgow had already achieved. Barcelona was a city ready to harness imaginative design. But so was Glasgow, and in Glasgow it was imaginative design that was directly commissioned by the community.

Five Spaces was a project of considerable complexity that involved five very different sites and five different partnerships between communities, artists and architects, as well as different sets of contractors, managed by ROCK DCM. It required that both social and creative issues be addressed. An additional factor was that schemes were carried out in areas that have experienced considerable deprivation and decay.

In all five of the areas in which the project created spaces during the course of 1999, the elements that make up the city have lost much of their diversity. Where once there would have been a mix of homes, workplaces and shops, the changing pattern of life which has had an impact on all contemporary cities has separated out these functions. Homes in isolation do not create a functioning city fabric. So the spaces created by the project were all conceived in various ways to fill that gap. All of them are linked to specific housing projects, and all of them attempt to encourage the social interaction that is an essential characteristic of a functional area of a city.

Deyan Sudjic, Director of Glasgow 1999

Page 2 and left: the opening of the Fruin Street play area in Possilpark.

Introduction

Few neighbourhoods can boast as prominent a position on the contemporary art scene as the ones that provide the sites for Glasgow 1999's Five Spaces project. Walk round what was once the derelict bowling green on Hawthorn's Fruin Street and you may be surprised to find a vast David Shrigley drawing scratched into the concrete surface of a playground. Just up the road at Saracen Cross the garden designed by Janet Hodgson is carefully constructed to mark the foundations of a non-existent building. Over to the West, in the district of Whiteinch, a huge beacon of light designed by Adam Barker-Mill illuminates an area where the famous shipyards once stood. In Govanhill, an underdeveloped plot of land next to the Larkfield Community Centre has been transformed, by Claire Barclay, into a beautifully constructed space to hold events. And in the East of the city, Kenny Hunter's sculpture of a calf is situated next to Judy Spark and Mike Hyatt's garden in the old Gallowgate cattle market.

These artworks form part of a larger initiative devised by Glasgow 1999 to transform some of Glasgow's urban 'gap sites' into spaces that bring a sense of community into the neighbourhoods. Urban gap sites are those neglected spaces that pock-mark a city. Overgrown and littered with rubbish, they can be bleak reminders of notorious housing policies, overburdened city councils and a lack of resources. Glasgow is no stranger to them. In the 1960s and 1970s, large sections of the city were cleared of tenement housing, leaving large areas of wasteland near to the city centre.

With funding from the Scottish Arts Council Lottery Fund, Scottish Homes, the Glasgow Development Agency and the URBAN European Initiative, Glasgow 1999 teamed up with five housing associations and the public art organisation Visual Art Projects. The sites were identified by the housing associations as places that could provide a focus for the existing local communities. Six artists paired up with architectural and landscape practices Zoo, Gross Max, Page and Park, Allan Murray and Christopher Platt to devise ways of developing new public spaces that would offer an attractive place for both local people as well as developing methods of construction in relation to regeneration.

The original idea was the result of a conversation between Pauline Gallacher, Initiatives Director of Glasgow 1999 and architect David Page. "It was a glimmer of something," Gallacher explains. "We both thought it would be wonderful if we could attract millennium lottery money into the city for a landscape project. The housing associations had made a big impact with high-quality new homes. Landscaping could reflect that achievement in the environment." They agreed that Glasgow's urban gap sites needed addressing and suggested a regeneration scheme. Their inspiration was based on a Barcelona initiative of the 1980s, when several spaces around the city were restructured and turned into parks, gardens and play areas. In Glasgow the circumstances were different; the spaces set the seal on a maturing rather than an emerging process of renewal. Glasgow 1999 acted as an umbrella organisation for the housing associations by distributing funds and managing the overall delivery of the scheme. Eleanor McAllister, Depute Director of Glasgow 1999, assumed the task of implementing the project: "We wanted to create a climate where professionals, policy makers and Glasgwegians in general would start looking hard at the nature of their streets, their park and their squares, and start asking for better things."

Visual Art Projects was appointed to manage the artists on behalf of Glasgow 1999 and the housing associations. "The artists, where possible, were selected by interviews on the basis of past practice", says Lucy Byatt from Visual Art Projects. "Some, like Claire Barclay at Govanhill, were funded by Glasgow 1999 to carry out an early stage research process." Barclay spent four months talking to residents and negotiating with Govanhill Housing Association. The chosen space was adjacent to the local community centre. The brief was to design a site where events could be held. A process like this was achieved in each space to enable the housing associations to work closely with the artists and architects, communicating their needs and aspirations.

Originally, the plan was to regenerate 15 sites but delays in funding meant that only five were possible in the time available. The organisation of the projects was quite a delicate and intricate issue. "It wasn't as if we had just commissioned five pieces of landscaping," says Gallacher. "It was much more than that". Their solution to potential logistical problems was to bring in construction management team ROCK DCM as main contractors and project managers. Mindful of the need to deliver as many local benefits as possible, ROCK DCM also implemented 23 placements for Glasgow Works, a programme designed to put long-term unemployed people back into work. Of the 23 Glasgow Workers almost all are now in full time employment. Those who are not are working on a pilot maintenance project for the spaces.

One of the core intentions for each space was that the artists would work in partnership with the rest of the design team. "It is important that it is made clear that we do not require the artists to become designers or honorary architects," says Byatt. "The two sorts of practices are different. The relationship that architects have to the meaning of their work differs. Artists, understandably, need control over the detail of their practice and this can be difficult to negotiate."

The schemes were promoted through the housing associations, which helped local people become involved in the process. Education Officer Wilma Eaton ran outreach projects in schools and local community centres in the five areas and invited the artists and architects to talk about their work. Zoo Architects presented their project to the kids of Possilpark with an outdoor slide show and David Shrigley devised a questionnaire for the children to fill in. Both were keen to glean information about what locals wanted for the site.

The success of the scheme was due to careful negotiation between all those concerned. "This was a very substantial investment in public space," says Byatt. "The project was under considerable scrutiny and there was a lot of pressure to succeed."

McAllister explains that "the housing associations were used to running projects themselves. They had a lot of experience of working with architects before, but less so with artists. We saw this as a very bold experiment."

Five Spaces was an opportunity to develop an integrated approach to design by drawing on different expertise. "Artists," explains Byatt, "have an important role to play. They, along with the rest of the design team, are not in the position to solve the social problems of an area, but they can be part of the process of highlighting the issues. The intention of the project was to enable the artists to have considerable influence, rather than to come up with an idea for a discreet object you might trip over."

The results have caused both delight and incredulity. At Possilpark the play area has been a success. There is a very clear sense of local ownership and support for the scheme thanks to local people working hard with the children to establish it as a safe place to be. The co-operative has invested in skipping ropes and other games equipment to encourage the process. According to Hawthorn Co-operative member Pauline Maguire, "There's one guy – we don't know his name – who's a skateboarder from Govanhill. He walked by the play area one evening and now comes over nearly every day to show the kids how to skateboard and use the ramp."

All the spaces have generated interest, not just in the local communities but elsewhere as well. McAllister hopes that this will encourage research into urban gap sites. "You can't just build good housing and leave a big barren space in between because the land is contaminated or there is a mineshaft. The fact is that most of Glasgow is a mix of industrial sites and big housing developments. The city will look gap-toothed if we don't recognise that." The hope is that Five Spaces sets a precedent, making way for other projects to continue after Glasgow 1999. Some are already in the pipeline. "The other housing associations here are very committed to the idea," says McAllister. "It would be great to see them succeed."

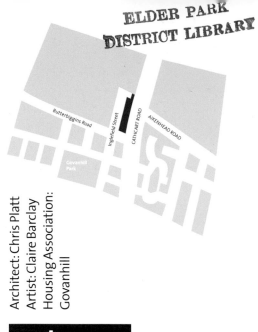

ELDER PARK
DISTRICT LIBRARY

Butterbiggins Road

Inglefield Street

CATHCART ROAD

AIKENHEAD ROAD

Govanhill
Park

Architect: Chris Platt
Artist: Claire Barclay
Housing Association:
Govanhill

1

Govanhill

The garden shed has become a potent
symbol in developed worlds. Often
seen as a male space, its function is
blurred. Is it a refuge? Is it used for
reflection? Or is it simply where you
store your plant pots? The artist
Claire Barclay, in collaboration with
architect Chris Platt and the Govanhill
Housing Association, has created a
Millennium Hut – a kind of modern
garden shed – which is a prominent
feature of the renovated area at
Larkfield Community Centre. Keen to
accomodate both public and private
interests, the project team consciously
designed their functional space to act
as a focus for the all the different
groups in the local area.

Prior to development, the wedge of
land on which the shed is sited was
under-developed; it was also situated
next to a busy main road. The
community centre was used, but its
surrounding land lay barren. Old
Govanhill was primarily a catchment
area for workers connected to

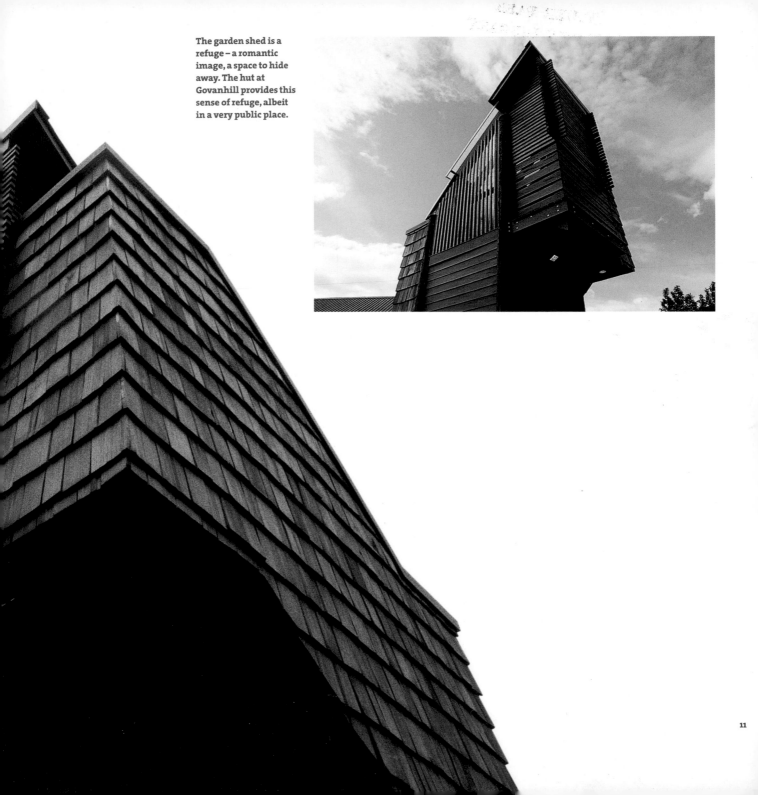

The garden shed is a refuge – a romantic image, a space to hide away. The hut at Govanhill provides this sense of refuge, albeit in a very public place.

11

The space, situated next to the Larkfield Community Centre, was built as a venue for local events and festivals (above right). Coloured poles were set into the stone to allow for attachments for canopies, which act as shelters in bad weather

Glasgow's long-standing coalmining industry. Now the area relies on service industries and small industrial works to provide employment. Govanhill Housing Association encompasses over 1500 houses with 70% of the residents on housing benefits.

Long term collaboration has been the hallmark of this project. Over two years ago, Claire Barclay was invited to exhibit in a tenement block in the area. What started as a site-specific exhibition grew into Barclay's wish to make something longer lasting. "I want to be part of a project that is changing the way spaces are used in the area."

The shed undoubtedly forms the focus on the regenerated space. Made from a variety of woods including oroco, pine and Douglas fir (salvaged from an airforce base in the Grampians), the three-storey building allows for storage of tools and gardening books, as well as a space for small plants to be seeded indoors. "We have consulted and collaborated with local groups and communities and recently had an open day to show them the future possibilities," says Ken MacDougal of Govanhill Housing Association. "There are plenty of groups, such as the camera club and the gardening club, that will make full use of the improved space. We would also like to see people using it as a performance venue – we have been in touch with local schools in the hope that they use it as such."

The area is designed for optimum daily use. At one end of the space, a series of different-coloured poles – constructed to allow for attachments for canopies – have been placed at intervals to provide a well-structured makeshift tent space for performances and events. At the other end, a beech hedge has been planted opposite the shed. "The overall project is about creating a space that is not a barrier," says Barclay. Surrounding the shed, the coloured poles and the planted areas are striped blocks of granite setts (paving blocks), laid in sections of two different colours; these elements combine to add a modern abstract graphic effect to the overall design of the scheme.

To the left of the shed is a doocot (dovecote), made from corrugated iron, that stands close to the fence behind the community centre. One of the few original features of the landscape to remain untouched, the doocot provides a neat metaphorical link between past and present, with its shape echoed by the new millennium hut. Fiercely guarded by its owner, with the help of local children, the doocot is a symbol of how areas with a function can bring people together.

The project has come about at a particularly special time."It is Govanhill Housing Association's 25th anniversary this year," says MacDougal, "so this project is a fitting way to celebrate our achievements. We hope that it will encourage other housing groups and local community groups to collaborate as well as we have done. It's the first time we have collaborated from the beginning with an artist – it proves that healthy debate can produce results. What is important about this project is that we are taking a long-term view. It is also part of a wider ongoing regeneration programme which includes the improvement of Govanhill Park."

The hut is supported by timber salvaged from an airforce base and houses gardening equipment, books and space to seed plants. It is hoped that local groups like the gardening club and the photographic society will use the shed for special projects.

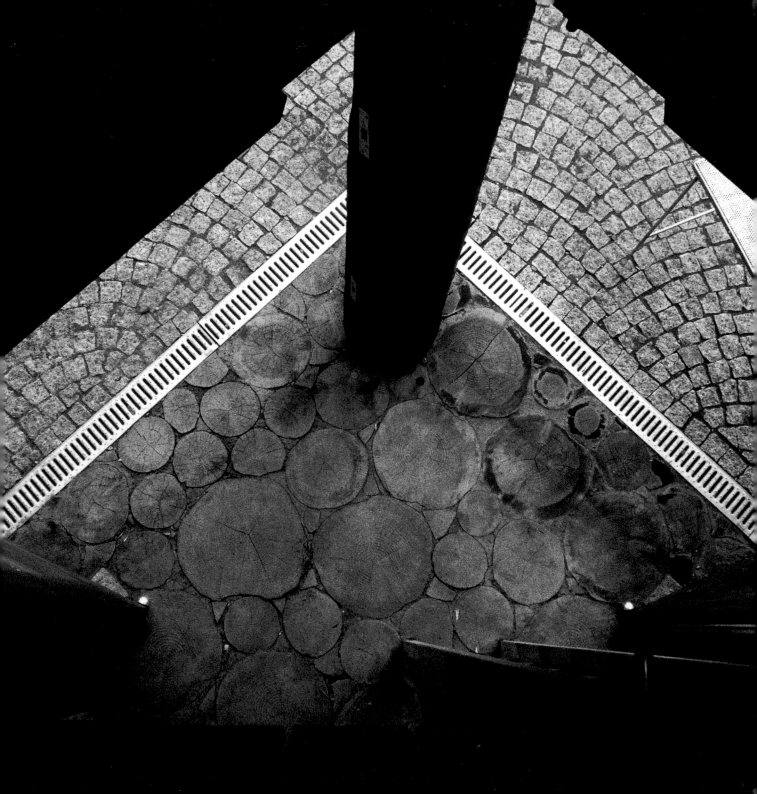

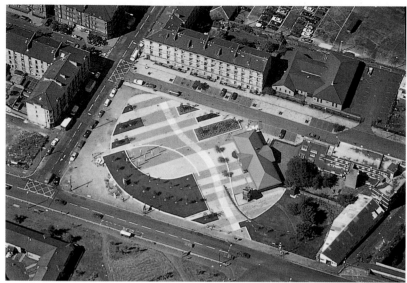

Seen from above, the graphic pattern created by Barclay's design for paving in three colours becomes clear.

Govanhill

To the south of the Clyde, beyond Gorbals and Hutchesontown, is the community of Govanhill. The major thoroughfare of Cathcart Road cuts directly through Govanhill, and acted as an important means of connection for the district when it first developed on the periphery of Glasgow during the 19th century. Industry was the key factor in Govanhill's growth. Intensive mining operations began when William Dixon arrived from Northumberland in 1771 and became the lessee of the Govan colliery. Dixon made a spectacular success of the business, at a time when coal was the vital fuel for steam power. After his death in 1822 his son, also William, continued the process of business expansion. The Govan Iron Works were established in 1839 to the south of Hutchesontown, and for decades afterwards the fiery glare of the furnaces inspired the famous nickname of 'Dixon's Blazes'.

Butterbiggins Road formed part of the route of the colliery's tramway track, which conveyed coal to the river Clyde. Inglefield House, on the northern boundary of Govanhill, was occupied by the manager of the Govan Iron Works, and the district was gradually built on to accommodate other members of Dixon's workforce. Their families probably worshipped at the Wesleyan Methodist chapel, which occupied the southern corner of Cathcart Road and Butterbiggins Road. The building no longer exists, although a substantial number of tenements survive as testimony to Govanhill's rapid expansion. From the late 1860s William Smith Dixon, representing the third generation of the coal and iron dynasty, laid out much of the area for residential development. As landowner, he demanded high standards, and today the Inglefield Street block beside the Govanhill 'gateway' serves as an early example of Dixon's favoured style of building.

Although adjacent to the city boundary, Govanhill was not part of Glasgow. However, population growth demanded more effective local government, and in 1877 the district was granted the semi-autonomous status of a 'police burgh' within Lanarkshire. Originally there were approximately 7,200 residents in Govanhill, but within ten years the number had increased to over 13,000. Many of the incomers were attracted by new industries established in the north-east of the district, notably Dubs & Company, which set up substantial railway workshops at Polmadie in 1865.

The burgh of Govanhill remained independent for only fourteen years. Like Possilpark, it was absorbed into Glasgow in 1891. While there was considerable unease about the loss of local identity, it was realised that the city could offer a range of services and amenities beyond the limited resources of the burgh. The district is now acknowledged to be one of Glasgow's most complete and distinctive late-Victorian tenement suburbs. Clearance was encouraged in some areas after the Second World War, with the result that rows of tenements to the east of Cathcart Road were demolished. Plans for an integrated road network in Glasgow meant that buildings were not necessarily replaced, although in the long term the city's ambitious highway strategy was curtailed.

The focus of industry in Govanhill also altered. The Govan Iron Works – the last blast furnace to operate within Glasgow – closed in 1958; and the Polmadie locomotive works closed in 1963. Yet throughout this period the district's population remained relatively stable. Moreover, from the 1950s Govanhill established a multi-ethnic profile, when Chinese and Pakistani communities began to settle. Continuity and change has therefore characterised Govanhill, which displays its history in its diversity of building styles.

Fruin Street
Possilpark

Architects: Zoo Architects
Artist: David Shrigley
Housing Association: Hawthorn

I was brought up in Possilpark
And see no reason to keep it dark
'Twas a clean and friendly place
with little strife
Where we helped one another to cope
with life
A close-knit community we were in fact
And tried to keep the clan intact...

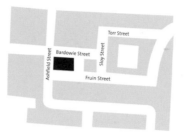

The site of Hawthorn's new play area had to be cleansed of chemical waste residue left by the old Saracen Foundry before building could commence. David Shrigley's drawings (opposite) and texts (overleaf) are sandblasted into the concrete floor.

So starts a poem called 'Nostalgia' by William Brown, a former councillor who spent his childhood in Possilpark. Walking around the area today, you can see how a sense of pride has dissolved in the face of problems related to unemployment and drug abuse. It wasn't always like this. As far back as the Roman period, Possil has been an important place; Agricola set up his main station house here in 81 AD. In 1847, Charles Dickens stayed at Possil House. The building formed part of the inspiration for his the author's semi-autobiographical novel 'David Copperfield'. Dickens called Possil the "Garden of the North... a relief from the general deprivation in Glasgow..."

When the Saracen Foundry closed in 1967 it provided blighted land for low-cost housing developments which aimed to relieve the problems of Glasgow's slums – unfortunately it only resulted in shifting the problems elsewhere. Now forming the site on which Hawthorn Housing Co-operative has been collaborating with Zoo Architects and artist David

Shrigley, Possil's land has been cleansed of the toxic chemical residue left by the foundry and turned into an urban garden.

As part of the research done for this project the collaborators undertook a survey, asking local children fundamental questions about their life as well as questions about their living environment: What don't you like about the place you live in? Describe your favourite landscape. Are you in a gang? Where is the furthest you have been from home? Do you do grafitti? Not surprisingly, there is not enough for kids to do in Possilpark. Many of

them welcomed the idea of a play area – be it in the form of trees, a climbing frame or a skateboard ramp. All of them hated the presence of drugs in the local area and saw the need for improvements.

Zoo sold the idea to the local kids with an outdoor slide show. "They loved it," said Zoo's Vivien Mason, "they understood completely because they're used to looking at computer games." The team then came up with some proposals that hope to ensure that the renovated space – about the size of a football pitch – will be more than just a place

in which to loiter, one in which children can enjoy themselves and learn at the same time.

David Shrigley has approached the project with characteristic humour. In one corner he has made a sandstone sculpture in the form of a pair of feet, set on a small plinth. The feet are shaped in such a way as to allow people to turn themselves into a piece of art by climbing into them. On the one hand a nod towards the need for art that can be both accessible and thought-provoking, and on the other a cheeky wink at the redundant nature of public statuary, Shrigley's piece neatly

summarises the problems inherent in creating public art in urban areas.

The survey highlighted the need to create a space that would inspire. Hence the play areas have been designed to ensure that the act of playing can also include the act of learning. In a section that is roughly 30 square metres, Shrigley has etched a map of Europe into the concrete with Hawthorn taking the place of Glasgow and ranking with Rome, Paris and Athens. Near to this is another map – this time a map of the stars. Made from a resin and glass aggregate, the design includes the Milky Way and other major constellations.

Keen to maintain a balance between form and content, the site contains special play areas found in more traditional parks – including a climbing wall and areas for younger children. Also incorporated here is a grafitti wall, and a special metal perimeter grille that ensures that roaming dogs are kept away.

This collaboration lays the foundations for an improved Possil. With its illustrious history and important heritage, the scheme forms a fitting beginning for the growth of a new community spirit.

Shrigley's stellar map (above) delineates the basketball zone. Witty plays on words by local children have begun to appear alongside the official inscriptions. A specially-created wall (overleaf) provides a legitimate canvas for graffiti

23

Saracen Cross and Fruin Street, Possilpark

Saracen Cross and the community of Possilpark originally lay outside Glasgow. The lands of Possil had several proprietors up to 1808, when the wealthy Campbell family of sugar merchants purchased and developed the estate.

Contemporary commentators remarked on the beauty of the wooded landscape, which served as the setting for Possil House, an 18th century mansion. After 1867 the estate was rapidly transformed by Walter Macfarlane, a Glasgow ironfounder, who needed room to expand his successful manufacturing business in sanitary, ornamental and architectural ironwork.

There was a historical connection between Macfarlane and James Graham of the Saracen's Head. In 1850 Macfarlane established his first foundry in Saracen Lane, on the site of the old inn. The Saracen Foundry remained in the Gallowgate until 1862, when it shifted west to Anderston.

Ten years later all of Macfarlane's business had relocated to the central part of the Possil estate. Macfarlane created the new community of Possilpark to accommodate his workforce. Saracen Street was laid out as shops and tenements, the thoroughfare leading directly north to the intricate, wrought-iron gates of the foundry. By the 1890s the firm employed 1,200 and the population of Possilpark had grown to 10,000. In the interim, other foundries were established in the vicinity, notably the Clydesdale Iron Works during the 1870s and the Keppoch and Possil Iron Works during the 1880s.

The products of the

Saracen Foundry were highly specialised and demand was such that Macfarlane & Company had become internationally renowned by the 1900s. However, the promotion of quality and craft skill co-existed uneasily with the environmental impact of heavy industry on the Possil district.

Indeed, during the 1880s one magazine witheringly referred to Macfarlane as 'the Laird of Fossiltown' because of the corrosion that smoke and other pollutants were causing.

In 1891 Glasgow's boundaries were substantially extended to include Possilpark.

The formal connection with the city was welcomed because of need for municipal services. Saracen Cross was at the heart of the development, at the junction of Saracen Street and Balmore Road. Not surprisingly, the

The bowling green (opposite) is now the site for Zoo Architects play ground. Below: The gates of Saracen Foundry

central feature was a Macfarlane clock-tower and fountain-trough. Yet Macfarlane's hopes to establish Possilpark as a model working-class community 'built entirely on modern principles' were overtaken by 20th century building developments. As a result, the character of the Cross has changed considerably, but a few of the original tenements still survive and have been recently refurbished.

Possilpark covered some 40 out of the 342 hectares of the Possil estate, which was substantially redeveloped for housing by Glasgow Corporation during the inter-war period. With over a million Glaswegians in one of Europe's most congested cities, there was government commitment to housing action in the wake of the First World War.

An early example of municipal initiative was at Hawthorn Street, to the east of the Saracen Foundry. Built under 1919 housing legislation, which granted state subsidies to local authorities, it represented the 'cottage' style of architecture regarded by contemporaries as the healthy alternative to claustrophobic tenements.

Despite the scale of housing activity in Possilpark, local industry contracted after the Second World War. Ornamental cast iron work fell out of fashion as stark

modernism replaced the ornate Victorian architectural style. By the 1960s all the larger concerns in the Possil district had disappeared. A symbolic link with the past was severed when the Saracen Foundry closed in 1967. The famous gates now adorn a recreation ground in Hawthorn. Industrial dereliction was compounded by profound social deprivation in parts of Possilpark, where unemployment levels reached over 60 per cent by the late 1980s.

At the same time, there was a strong sense of community identity, which did not dissolve in the aftermath of deindustrialisation.

Municipal support of housing rehabilitation was combined with organised community efforts to improve the environment and help Macfarlane's 'Fossiltown' flourish again.

3 Saracen Cross

Architects: Allan Murray Architects
Artist: Janet Hodgson
Landscape Architect: Amanda Stokes
Horticulturalist: James Hitchmough
Housing Association: Springburn and Possilpark

Prior to this project, Saracen Cross was a neglected public space. It is at the edge of an important new housing development planned for the future. The garden uses the materials of a building site as if the foundations have been started but no more. In the spring, colourful plants will emerge.

For centuries, Saracen Cross has been a crossroads, historically for the old coaching routes that ran through Glasgow. In the 18th century the area lay on the boundaries of the Possil Estate. Land was slowly sold off to house the Victorian economic growth and at the height of the Industrial Revolution Saracen Cross was an internationally important area which housed vast industrial factories that Processed the raw materials for locomotives. However, a decline in demand after World War II led to a severe collapse. Unemployment increased and the area fell into delapidation. Despite the decline, however, there has always been an overwhelming sense of pride among the community – knowing that it was this small corner of Glasgow that was part of some of the greatest engineering feats of the century.

"Talking to some of the local

historians, you can sense that this pride has not disappeared," says Allan Murray, the architect of the Saracen Cross project. Before the development, Saracen Cross had been left as a barren site, used as a walk-through space from the housing estates to Saracen Street. Now it has been divided into two sections, one section designed by Allan Murray Architects and the other by Janet Hodgson, a London-based artist, who has been working in collaboration with horticulturalist James Hitchmough and the landscape architect, Amanda Stokes.

Allan Murray's approach has been in response to the architectural and industrial heritage of the area. "The floorscape has been designed to allude to the work that was going on at the foundry, borne out in the fluidity of the area. We have also included stone seating to break up the space." As well as introducing a series of stone bollards, to demarcate the area from the residential sites adjacent, a flank of trees has been planted. "It is a very permeable space," says Murray, "people can flow through the space if they are passing through, or they can sit down and watch the world go by."

Janet Hodgson's project takes its lead from the hard landscaping. This scheme, which develops one half of the existing 1960s square, proposes a future development to finish the square sometime within the next five years. For this reason Janet Hodgson has chosen to work on the edge of the new square, on the site of a proposed four-storey building which will eventually form the final side of the development. Using the footprint of the building to come, Hodgson,

Planting bulbs (left) in one of the cages at the opening event for Saracen Cross.

working with Stokes and Hitchmough, has planted a garden and created a job for a local gardener to last for a minimum of three years. As Janet explained: "I wanted to provide guaranteed through-care for the site rather than an artwork."

The garden, resembling a building site, is a complex mixture of herbaceous perennials and formal hedging. Set within cast concrete walkways, the gravel beds in the shape of rooms contain herbaceous planting that enlarges upon or exaggerates the character of the wild plants that already exist on the gap sites around the square. In the garden the thistles will be silver and six feet tall and interspersed with giant orange poppies and blue daisies. Metal cages in the shape of rooms and walls contain the hedging.

The garden is, in many ways, experimental; an intentionally

vulnerable intervention into a difficult area, where conventional wisdom would be to provide an indestructible environment. Instead the garden creates a small but conspicuous area which is continually cared for and maintained.

Hitchmough and Stokes felt the need for a new direction to a public collaboration. "We wanted to move away from the more austere approach to public projects. We wanted to create something with a scale similar to someone's back garden, rather than a plaza garden. Hence we chose plants that would be familiar but designed it in such a way that it would be more provocative. We have taken the idea of

the building to come – in the shape of the ground plan fitting. So there are no masonry walls. We have built in these hedge-like structures, encased in steel cages two and a half metres tall, placed in rhythmical sequences. It is very much following the idea of Derek Jarman's cottage at Dungeness, turning the space into something with a sacred element."

"It will make a difference to the area in a subtle way," says David Sherry, from Springburn and Possilpark Housing Association. "It's a reflection of our industrial heritage which we must keep alive. Even though it is a fairly small change, it is a welcome one. We have been involved very closely with

local residents and local gardening clubs will be involved. Those who are maintaining it will be from a community training organisation."

Saracen Cross is a major pedestrian through-way linking the large housing estates which lie on the periphery of Saracen Street. What was once a barren wasteland that collected nothing but litter is now the floral focus – a neat metaphor for the future growth and regeneration in Possilpark.

Whiteinch Cross

Landscape Architects: Gross.Max
Artist: Adam Barker-Mill
Housing Association: Whiteinch and
Scotstoun Housing Association

4

Whiteinch Cross, like Saracen Cross, has a strong historical identity. Here, when Glasgow was a growing town, Whiteinch Cross was a popular resting place for travellers and somewhere where they could water their horses. Fast forward a couple of hundred years, through Glasgow's heavy industrial period to the present day, and the Cross is the first spot you arrive at on emerging from the Clyde Tunnel. If you're on the number 62 bus going down the Dumbarton Road, passing by the exit from the tunnel, then you won't miss Adam Barker-Mill's construction – a ten metre tower made from white pigmented cast concrete with a west facing slit that beams a solitary but piercing light. It forms the most immediately visual focus for the regenerated area that comprises of three separate interlinking sections – a park, a square and a promenade.

Facing Vishna's Central Store, the local nerve centre for Irn Bru and WagonWheel purchases, the new park has used the existing green strip of trees and incorporated a steel curb,

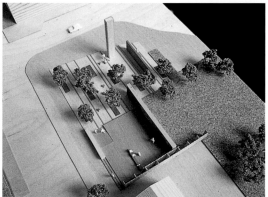

Whiteinch has always been a place for travellers to rest. The architects have used this history to create a space where people can relax and watch the world go by. A model of the site (left) built by Zoo Architects demonstrates how Adam Barker-Mill's light tower provides an emphatic focus for the scheme. The tower (right) is designed to act as a beacon that can be seen for miles around.

DUMBARTON ROAD

Northinch Street

Squire Street

Smith Street

Whiteinch Cross

According to a map of the West of Scotland published by the Dutch firm of W. & J. Blaeu in 1654, Whiteinch was one of several islands existing in the channel of the Clyde to the west of Glasgow. Over time the course of the river changed and Whiteinch was absorbed into the north bank. By the early 19th century the area was largely farmland. However, an augury of changing times was the establishment of Tod & McGregor's shipyard in the neighbouring village of Partick, where the first all-iron steamer was launched in 1835. Twenty years later Whiteinch became a fully-fledged shipbuilding community when the firm of Barclay Curle & Company founded their Clydeholm yard. An extensive enterprise, dating back to 1818, Barclay Curle specialised in quality ocean liners and passenger vessels, notably for the East India and transatlantic routes.

The rapid industrialisation of the north-west bank of the Clyde was the main reason for the creation of the police burgh of Partick in 1852. Whiteinch formed part of this new administrative entity, and the burgh grew from a population of 5,000 to over 66,800 in 1911. Although retaining its autonomous character far longer than Govanhill, Partick became part of Glasgow in 1912. After a prolonged and expensive campaign by the city's civic rulers, the community eventually agreed to annexation. Even today the 60-year legacy of burgh government lingers in certain Whiteinch street titles. For instance, in 1900 the commissioners named Smith Street in honour of James Parker Smith, Liberal Unionist MP for Partick and proprietor of the nearby estate of Jordanhill. Another wealthy social activist with a paternalistic interest in Whiteinch was Thomas Corbett, who in 1877 erected Summerfield Cottages next to the Cross as 'model workmen's dwellings'. The neat row of terraced houses still exists, adding to the eclectic mixture of architectural styles that distinguish the area.

However, like so many areas of Glasgow from the late 19th century, tenements were the favoured form of housing in Whiteinch. Although building standards were generally high, the district's strategic location next to the river meant that living conditions could be crowded. By the First World War the demand for housing had become so high that the government was forced to pass rent restriction legislation in an attempt to stop excessive charges by profiteering landlords.

Warship production after 1914 was a wholly new direction for Barclay Curle, which hitherto had engaged solely in merchant shipbuilding, engineering and repairing. It was a particularly difficult market to keep stable during the inter-war depression, although by this time the Whiteinch firm had been taken over by the Tyneside-based shipbuilders, Swan Hunter & Wigham Richardson. To some extent this business connection helped Barclay Curle to survive and cushioned the impact of unemployment on Whiteinch, especially during the black years of the early 1930s. However, in the longer term the increased preference for air travel fatally undermined the company's market for passenger shipping. By 1967 shipbuilding had ceased in the Clydeholm yard, and the site was transformed into an industrial estate.

The construction of the Clyde tunnel, linking the north and south banks of the river, substantially altered the urban landscape of the area. The tunnel became operational in 1964, after generating considerable controversy because of the incursion of the northern access road into the amenity area of Victoria Park. The Clydeside Expressway opened in the 1980s, and compounded the sense of fragmentation as it cut through the heart of Whiteinch. The Five Spaces initiative has helped to redress this by offering locals a community base.

The architects used frames made from Cor-ten steel plates. The walls are designed to change colour as the weather changes.

while an abstract but rhythmic pattern of red and green 'airport runway' lights illuminate the park at night, the green reflecting against the concrete, the red projecting skywards.

The square incorporates the most architectural intervention of the project. Situated at the corner of Smith Street and Dumbarton Road, it has become a new place for rest and relaxation in an area which could only previously offer a solitary toilet. After consultation with local groups and Whiteinch and Scotstoun Housing Association, the landscape architects Gross.Max felt that Glasgow's iron and steel building heritage could be reflected in several aspects of the new garden. Consequently, two free-standing frames made from galvanised steel, clad with Cor-ten steel plates are a visual reminder of the raw materials used in Glasgow's heavy industrial practice, from shipbulding to locomotives. In an attempt to soften the landscape, the walls change colour according to the weather – from a deep, rich orange on sunny days to a dark iron red on the more rainy days. On one

of the walls, a curtain of water running eight metres long cascades from top to bottom – a modern reinterpretation of the historic function of the Cross. In a modern interpretation of the pergola, two galvanised steel frames will eventually be festooned with wisteria.

Divided into two levels, the lower level contains a new section of trees enclosed in cast iron grilles to allow unhampered growth. Fixed around these at various points are black chairs made from polished reinforced concrete. The upper level is dominated by honey-coloured Clashach sandstone slabs, taken from a small quarry on the Moray Firth. The architects invited the artist Adam Barker-Mill to design a light installation to complement their designs and arrived at his light tower. "I wanted to create a beacon for the area, so chose a light tower that could be seen from far away," says Barker-Mill. "It complements the airport runway lights that are in place at ground level, giving the area a sense of continuity."

After consultation with local residents, Barker-Mill decided his tower

would be better if painted white. "Concrete is a dirty word in Glasgow. For the residents it represented the architectural disasters of the 1960s, epitomised by the tower blocks that are scattered across the city."

The new site is an improvement according to Jim Calderwood from the Housing Association. "People either love or hate it. It is unconventional in its design. I think in these situations, it is always a good idea to take the long term view. This is part of an investment into the area and it may well attract further capital. As it is now, it is being used on a regular basis."

The collaborators in this project have turned a space that had lost its function and transformed it into a working park. The combination of the lofty light tower, which acts as a new beacon for the area, and the landscaped garden with soft and hard features, brings part of the area to life. In contemporary urban environments where leisure is becoming increasingly linked to commerce, this renovated space offers a rare place in the city to time out from the daily grind.

Graham Square
Gallowgate

5

Architects: Page and Park Architects
Artists: Kenny Hunter, Judy Spark
Landscape Architect: Mike Hyatt
Housing Association: Molendinar Park

Kenny Hunter's 'Golden Calf' will be sited on ground level at the rear of Graham Square (below). It links Gallowgate's past life as a cattle market with its new begining as a residential area. Overleaf: Hunter at work on the sculpture

Billy Connolly made Gallowgate famous again in the 1970s with a modern interpretation of The Last Supper. The scene was the Saracen's Head, one of the best-known pubs in the east end. Here it was, said Connolly, that Jesus spoke to his followers, albeit with a poke of chips and a couple of pints. Despite the joke, Connolly knew how important Gallowgate is to Glasgow and not just because of its close proximity to Glasgow's contemporary version of a city cathedral; Celtic's football stadium, Parkhead.

Today it is being transformed into a new inner city landscape with the help of the recently-created Molendinar Park Housing Association. Historically it was very different. The Gallowgate is the second oldest street in the city, forming as it did one of the central axes of the rapidly growing area. From the very beginning, it had always been used as a meeting point for animal drovers. The Drovers Arms still stands, close to the new development at Graham Square. As the name suggests, Gallowgate was once also the site for public executions. However it was the

Graham Square

Graham Square is located off Glasgow's Gallowgate, a famous east end thoroughfare with origins stretching back at least to the 14th century. About 1770 James Graham, owner of the Saracen's Head Inn, acquired the ground with a view to building houses that would attract better-off Glaswegians.

Graham hoped to profit from Glasgow's building boom during the late 18th century. There was demand for property as the population increased rapidly, rising from 23,500 inhabitants to over 77,300 by 1801. However, Graham Square proved to be too ambitious a project for its proprietor. His building standards did not meet the expectations of prospective purchasers and the area was considered remote from the town centre. Graham accumulated considerable debt because of the failed development. He died in 1777, leaving his widow Jean Leckie to pay off his creditors and make her name independently as the formidable landlady of the Saracen's Head.

The future for the Square was not residential but industrial. George Grant and his sons set up their substantial powerloom factory in Graham Square between 1825 and 1845. Yet although this created jobs, there were also disturbing social consequences. Problems associated with pollution and inadequate housing conditions began to intensify, with parts of the area identified as grossly overcrowded.

In 1818 the cattle market was moved to grounds adjoining Graham Square. At the time the market was lauded as the largest outside Smithfield in London, although by the end of the century the scale of operations was such that the area had increased to 29,263 square metres. Feeding the people was a massive business, as Glasgow accommodated over three quarters of a million inhabitants in 1901, ranking it as the sixth largest city in Europe.

In its heyday the market dealt not only in live cattle, but pigs, sheep and goats. Graham Square was the focal point of the thriving west of Scotland meat trade, and contained a hotel to serve the needs of visiting farmers, breeders, butchers and dealers.

Customer demand in a city of over a million people from 1912 meant that business remained buoyant, despite the vicissitudes of war and industrial depression. Activity only slowed down when controls were imposed by the Ministry of Food during the rationing period of 1940 to 1954, and the movement of animals was restricted.

Gallowgate altered fundamentally after the post-war period when Glasgow Corporation consolidated slum clearance. As part of the city's development plan, the district was identified as suitable for wholesale restructuring and most of the tenements were demolished. Between 1951 and 1971 the population fell from 26,200 to 11,700. During this period Glasgow's industry was decimated, notably the long-standing staples of iron and steel, which was an important base of the local economy. De-industrialisation contributed to the decline of the area around Graham Square. By 1976 the problem had reached such critical proportions that the Glasgow Eastern Area Renewal (GEAR) project was set up, in the hope of breathing new life into what remained of the east-end community.

A particularly successful GEAR achievement during the eleven years of the project was the rehabilitation of existing tenements and new building. Job creation proved to be more problematic, given the acutely depressed climate of the times. Meanwhile, the meat market was itself run down, and business was gradually transferred to new premises at Duke Street. By the early 1990s the site was no longer used, except for car auctions.

Glasgow's famous 'Barras' market (below) uncharacteristically devoid of people.

41

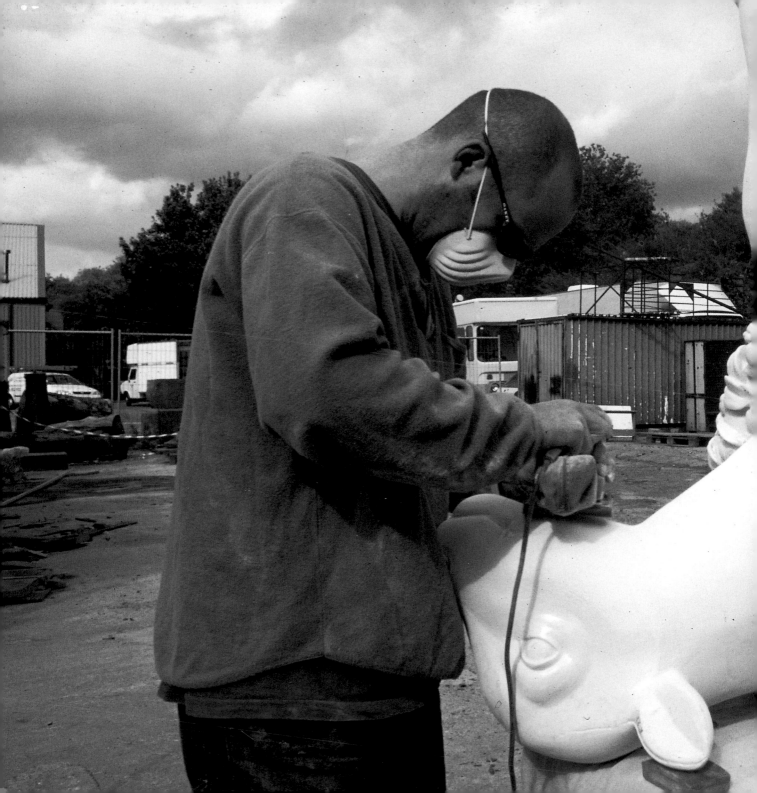

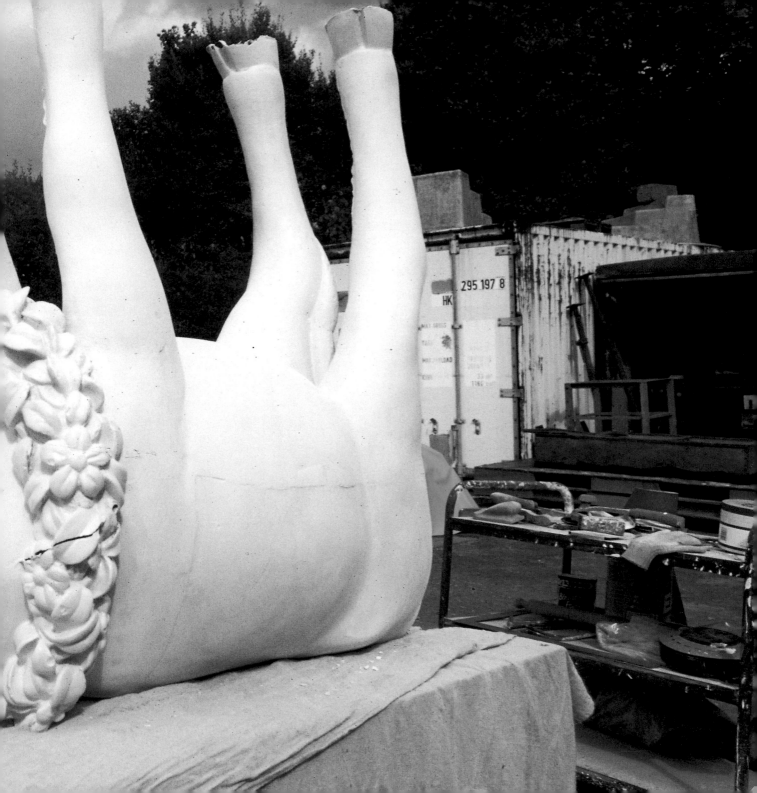

The new housing development includes buildings by architects Page and Park (above). A drawing by landscape architect Mike Hyatt (right) illustrates the thinking behind the plans for Judy Spark's garden.

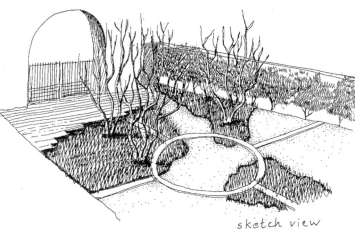

sketch view

Victorians who, instead of using it as a human execution ground, turned to animals instead, building an extensive meat market. Designed by John Carrick and built in the neo-classical style back in 1875, it epitomised a new civic pride, resplendent with gargoyles in the form of heads of cattle and rams. Today the abattoir has moved a few blocks downwind and only the façade of this listed building remains intact. It is the façade that forms the focus of Molendinar's regeneration programme, which is divided into three sections.

The first lies in the main square just off Gallowgate. Here the footpaths and carriageways have been paved in Caithness stone, the kerbs in granite. The second section of the square is the main urban space. Here architects Page and Park have constructed the Matador Building close to the meat market façade. "We wanted to respond to the past function of the area. The Matador's Building has curved fins to represent the matador's cloak confronting the listed façade – which is the symbol for the bull." Continuing with the theme, artist Kenny Hunter has placed a white sculpture of a calf on a plinth. "My piece has a symbolic title," says Hunter. "It is called the Golden Calf, to reflect a society in doubt. There are plenty of other meanings you could attach to it though. On a fairly simplistic level it represents the extent to which we have lost touch with animals these days, treating them as we do more as packaged commodities. On a more historical level, the piece links the old and the new, reminding us of what the area was once used for." Hunter has been strongly influenced by the

changing role of public statuary and is keen make us aware that times have changed. "Glasgow has a strong history of public art, but nowadays the emphasis is shifting over to the role of artist as facilitator, and changing the role of the audience away from that of the passive spectator. It is all about being aware of a collective responsibility, which is what this project is all about."

Rob Joiner from the Moledinar Housing Association would agree. "We are doing something new here. At present we don't really have a local community, as we are creating a new

area from past dereliction. We own 114 houses while new houses are being built all the time by architects that include Richard Murphy and Page and Park. The collaborative element of the project is one way of attracting new residents to the area."

The third section of the project is the Orchard Garden, a semi-private space enclosed by a high wall. A soft landscape with small trees, it is the site of artist Judy Spark's project. Here she has built concrete structures that have been attached to the perimeter wall. "I worked with a landscape architect to create what is a bit like a large scale installation. It has been a strange community project as we have not met the people who are intending to move in. It has been a bit like doing a consultation with a ghost population. Gallowgate has never had a good reputation, so this garden is a chance to change things. I have used plants that have a Zen-like quality to them to give a sense of tranquillity." Spark has chosen moss taken from around the city and transplanted it using a special mounted culture process that includes using silicone. "Using different kinds of Glasgow moss is relevant," says Spark. It mirrors the diversity of the people who might be moving into the area. There is also a risk element involved in this project as it will be a while before we determine whether the moss is going to grow successfully, whether it will adapt to its new environment. It is a metaphor for the project as a whole."

Artists

Claire Barclay
Born in Paisley, 1968
Glasgow School of Art
Selected solo exhibitions
1997 'Out of the Woods',
Centre for Contemporary
Art, Glasgow
1997 'Museum Intervention',
Tasmanian Museum and
Art Gallery, Hobart
1997 'Claire Barclay, New
works', Plimsol Gallery,
Hobart
1998 'Dream Catcher',
Melbourne, Australia
Selected group exhibitions
1994 'The Institute of
Cultural Anxiety', Glasgow
1995 'The Cube', Canberra
Contemporary Art Space,
Canberra
1996 'Girls High', Old
Fruitmarket, Glasgow;
Institute of Contemporary
Arts, London
1997 'Seeing Hozomeen',
Collective Gallery,
Edinburgh
1997 'Nerve', Glasgow
Projects; Artspace, Sydney
1997 'Clean and Sane',
Stockholm
1997 'Hong Kong Island',
Transmission Gallery,
Edinburgh
1998 'If I ruled the world',
The Living Art Museum,
Reykjavik
1998 'A Still Volcano Life',
South Gallery, Sydney

Adam Barker-Mill
Born in Somerset, 1940
Magdalen College, Oxford
London School of Film
Technique, Brixton
Selected solo exhibitions
1988 'SpaceLight 1', ANTA,
London
1989 'SpaceLight 2', Issey

Miyake, London
1991 'Light works', Ikon
Corporation, London
1992 '3 Columns', Victoria
Miro Gallery, London
1997 'Photosynthesis',
Inverleith House, Edinburgh
Selected group exhibitions
1985 'Who's afraid of red,
yellow and blue?', Arnolfini,
Bristol
1990 'Between Dimensions',
Curwen Gallery, London
1993 'Light Installations',
Riverside One, London
1996 'Northern Lights',
Fruitmarket Gallery,
Edinburgh
1996 'Light: an exhibition',
Sainsbury Centre, Norwich

Janet Hodgson
Born in Bolton, 1960
Wimbledon School of Art
Selected solo exhibitions
1996 'this was like that now
it's like this', The
Cornerhouse,
Middlesbrough
1998 'The History Lesson',
Bluecoat Gallery, Liverpool
1998 'Every picture tells a
story', Photo 98, Leeds;
General Hospital, Leeds
Selected group exhibitions
1993 'Heatwave', Serpentine
Gallery, London
1994 'On Location', Bluecoat
Gallery, Liverpool
1995 'Making It', Tate Gallery,
Liverpool
1996 'East International',
Norwich School of Art
1998 'artranspennine98'
(exhibition across the
Transpennine region)
Publications
1998 *Public:Art:Space*,
Merrell Holberton, London
1999 *The History Lesson*,

Bluecoat Gallery, Liverpool
1999 *Leaving Tracks:
artranspennine98*, August
Media, London

Kenny Hunter
Born in Edinburgh, 1962
Glasgow School of Art
Selected solo exhibitions
1994 'Nexus', Lycee de Jaques
Prevert, Longjumeau, France
1996 'Churchill's Dogs',
Norwich Gallery, Norwich
1998 Leeds Metropolitan
University Gallery, Leeds
1998 Arnolfini, Bristol
1998 Modern Art Inc,
London
1999 National Portrait
Gallery, Edinburgh
Group exhibitions
1993 'East', Norwich School
of Art, Norwich
1993 'Fuse', Collins Gallery,
Glasgow
1995 SWARM, toured
through Scotland
1997 'Blueprint', Glasgow
Print Studio, Glasgow
1997 'The Lost Ark', Centre for
Contemporary Arts,
Glasgow
1998 'Ark', Travelling Gallery,
Edinburgh
1999 'The Multiple Store',
Institute of Contemporary
Arts, London
Publications
1998 *Kenny Hunter*,
Arnolfini, Bristol
1999 *Exhibition Guide*, The
Scottish National Portrait
Gallery, Edinburgh

David Shrigley
Born in Macclesfield, 1968
Glasgow School of Art
Selected solo exhibitions
1995 'Map of the Sewer'
Transmission Gallery,

Glasgow
1996 Catalyst Arts, Belfast
1997 Hermetic Gallery,
Milwaukee
1997 Centre for
Contemporary Arts,
Glasgow
1997 Photographers Gallery,
London
1998 Bloom Gallery,
Amsterdam
1999 Stephen Friedman
Gallery, London
Group exhibitions
1994 'Some of my Friends'
Gallerie Campbells
Occasionally, Copenhagen
1995 'Scottish Autumn'
Bartok 32 Galeria, Budapest
1996 'Sarah Staton
Superstore', Up & Co., New
York
1997 'Blueprint', De Appel,
Amsterdam
1998 'Surfacing', Institute of
Contemporary Arts, London
1998 'Habitat', Centre for
Contemporary Photography,
Melbourne
1999 'Waste Management',
Art Gallery of Ontario,
Toronto
Publications
1992 *Merry Eczema*, Black
Rose, Glasgow
1994 *Blanket of Filth*, Armpit
Press, Glasgow
1991 *Slug Trails*, Black Rose,
Glasgow
1995 *Enquire Within*, Armpit
Press, Glasgow
1996 *Drawings Done Whilst
on Phone to Idiot*, Armpit
Press, Glasgow
1996 *Err*, Bookworks, London
1996 *Let Not These Shadows
Fall Upon Thee*, Tramway,
Glasgow
1998 *Why we got the sack
from the Museum*, The

Redstone Press, London
1998 *To Make Meringue You Must Beat the Egg Whites until they look like this*, Nicolai Wallner, Copenhagen
1998 *Centre Parting*, The Little Cockroach Press, Toronto
1998 *Blank Page and Other Pages*, The Modern Institute, Glasgow

Judy Spark
Born in Glasgow, 1965
Glasgow School of Art
Selected exhibitions
1996 'Fuse', Maclellan Galleries, Glasgow
1996 'Wileczka', Galeria State, Krakow, Poland
1997 'Non de la Rambla', Las Ramblas, Barcelona
1997 'Resound', Highland Park Distillery, Orkney Islands
1998 'Wallpaper Video', Christchurch, New Zealand
1998 'Lapland', British Council, Edinburgh
1998 'This Island Earth', An Turieann Arts Centre, Isle of Skye
Publications
1994 *New Art in Scotland*, Centre for Contemporary Arts, Glasgow
1996 *Ceriphs*, Patrick Macklin
1996 *The City and the River*, Royal Institute of British Architects, London
1996 *Fuse*, Glasgow
1998 *SHAVE*, Artists catalogue
1998 *Dangerous Ground*, Public Art Conference, Glasgow

Architects

Gross. Max
Established in 1995
Selected projects
1992-98 Sandveien Housing Estate, Lerwick, Shetland Islands
1995 Two parks at Potsdammer Platz, Berlin
1996 Hannover Expo 2000
1999 Earth Centre, Doncaster
Exhibitions
1994 'Beyond the Bypass', Edinburgh College of Art, Edinburgh
1996 'Manifesto', Edinburgh
1999 '12+ SKY', Kelvingrove Museum, Glasgow

Dr James Hitchmough
1979 BSc Horticulture
1983-93 Lecturer at University of Melbourne
Current Reader and Director of the Research School, Dept of Landscape, University of Sheffield.

Allan Murray Architects
Established in 1992
Selected projects
1996 Peterhead Maritime Centre, Aberdeen
1997 The MacRobert Arts Centre, Stirling
1998 Hamilton Arts Centre, Hamilton
1998 Greenside, Edinburgh
1999 Site A1, Edinburgh Park, Edinburgh
Awards
1995 Scottish Architectural Award for Best Building of the Year
1998 Royal Scottish Academy's Medal for Architecture

Page and Park Architects
Established in 1981
Selected projects
1991 Italian Centre, Glasgow
1991 St Mungo Museum, Glasgow
1995-7 The Royal Mile, Edinburgh
1996-7 Municipal Building, Port Glasgow
1996 St Francis Church and Friary, Glasgow
1999 The Lighthouse, Scotland's Centre for Architecture, Design and the City, Glasgow
Awards
1990 Scottish Civic Trust Award Scheme
1993 Award for St Mungo Museum
1995 Royal Institute of British Architects Award
1998 Glasgow Institute of Architects Award

Karen Pickering
(Architect and Associate with Page and Park)
Selected projects
1991 Detailed design for fit-out of St Mungo Museum, Glasgow
1991 Urban strategy study for development of Sneddon Area, Paisley
1992 Project Architect on traffic calming and related schemes, Royal Mile, Edinburgh.
1997 Project Architect for St Francis Church and Friary, Glasgow
Awards
1990 Royal Scottish Academy Travel Scholarship
1998 Competition-winning new build housing for Molendinar Housing Association

Christopher Platt Architect
Established in 1997
Awards
1996 Scottish Architectural Award for Best Architect

John Richards (Landscape Consultancy)
MA Landscape Architecture
Established 1994

Amanda Stokes
MA Landscape Architecture
Established 1999

Zoo Architects
Established in 1994
Selected projects
1994 187 Old Rutherglen Road, Glasgow
1997 Arts project, Tramway, Glasgow
1997 Public Realm, Manchester Street, Liverpool
1998 Housing-Living sites, Royal Institute of British Architects.
1998 Royston Music Project, Glasgow
1998 Design Capsule, Glasgow
1999 Wee People's City, Glasgow
1999 Todd Building, Glasgow
Awards
1997 RSA Award, Public Realm, Manchester Street, Liverpool

Glasgow 1999
UK City of Architecture and Design

GLASGOW 1999 MANAGMENT TEAM

Deyan Sudjic Director
Eleanor McAllister Depute Director
Nicole Bellamy Exhibitions Director
Pauline Gallacher Community Initiatives Director
Sarah Gaventa Communications Director
Andrew Gibb Development Director
Gordon Ritchie Marketing Manager
Anne Wallace Education Officer
Bruce Wood Glasgow Collection Director

THE FIVE SPACES TEAM

Eleanor McAllister Depute Director, 1999 and Capital Projects Manager
Pauline Gallacher Initiatives Director
Kirsteen McCrury Grants and Finance Officer
Maureen O'Rourke Administrative Assistant

CONSULTANTS

Rock DCM
Norrie Innes
Michael Kelly
David McAllister
Visual Art Projects
Lucy Byatt
Julia Radcliffe
Ben Spencer

FUNDERS

Glasgow Development Agency
Glasgow City Council (Contributions made to development costs via the core Glasgow 1999 budget)
Scottish Arts Council
Ian Gilzean
Scottish Homes
Alistair Dickson
Andrew Fyfe
Hunter Reid
Urban European Initiative

COLLABORATORS

Glasgow City Council Land Services
Brian Atkinson
Bert de Jong
Roads and Property Services
Glasgow City Council Physical and Economic Regeneration
Don Bennett
Michael Hayes
Riccardo Marini
Judith Parsons
Glasgow City Council Protective Services
Elaine Galletly
Greater Easterhouse Development Company
Neil Gaffney
Bob Laverty
Glasgow Works
Bob Marshall

HOUSING ASSOCIATIONS

Govanhill Housing Association
Lyn Ewing
Robert Farrell
Kenneth MacDougall
Ann Scott
Hawthorn Housing Co-operative
Craig Adair
Betty Anderson
Susan Brown
Sally Little
David McKenzie
Molendinar Housing Association
Professor J Dickson
Michael Fletcher
Rob Joiner
Kenny MacKay
Powder Hall Bronze
Pat Wolsley
Springburn and Possilpark Housing Association
Euan Barr
Eddie Donaldson (Secretary of the Housing Association for more than 20 years, who sadly did not live to see the space completed)
Bobby Fleming
Dave Sherry
Robert Tamborini
Whiteinch and Scotstoun Housing Association
Jim Calderwood
Catherine MacAulay
Christina Madden
Peter McClymont
John Ross
Sandy Urquhart

Thanks to all the staff and committee members of the housing associations whose spaces could not proceed (Reidvale, New Gorbals, Camlachie, Partick, Glen Oaks and Tollcross), for their enthusiasm for the project. We hope the realisation of the Five Spaces will renew their ambitions for their own projects.

SUPPORTERS

Hildebrand Frey at the Urban Design Studies Unit, Department of Architecture, University of Strathclyde;
Enric Miralles and the city of Barcelona, who inspired us to strive for great things;
David Page of Page and Park Architects, who came up with the original concept for Five Spaces;
SHARE (Scottish Housing Associations Resources for Education)